Contents

Any words appearing in the text in bold, **like this**, are explained in the glossary.

Meet the arachnids

As night falls across the Californian desert, thousands of scorpions and tarantulas crawl out of their hiding places to hunt. They wait in silence. Any insect that disturbs the sand will be killed with a deadly bite or sting.

Tarantulas and scorpions are **predators**. They survive by hunting and eating other animals. Every part of a predator's body is designed to help it find, catch, and eat meat.

Tarantulas are also called bird-eaters. They are the world's largest spiders.

In Mexico, more than 100 people are killed by scorpions every year.

4

ANIMALS HEAD TO HEAD

SCORPION VS. Tarantula

This book is dedicated to the memory of Lucy Owen, who really cared about this series.

ISABEL THOMAS

www.raintreepublishers.co.uk
Visit our website to find out more information about **Raintree** books.

To order:
☎ Phone 44 (0) 1865 888112
🖹 Send a fax to 44 (0) 1865 314091
🖥 Visit the Raintree bookshop at **www.raintreepublishers.co.uk** to browse
our catalogue and order online.

First published in Great Britain by Raintree,
Halley Court, Jordan Hill, Oxford OX2 8EJ,
part of Harcourt Education.
Raintree is a registered trademark
of Harcourt Education Ltd.

© Harcourt Education Ltd 2006
First published in paperback in 2007.
The moral right of the proprietor has been asserted.

Editorial: Dan Nunn and Katie Shepherd
Design: Victoria Bevan
and Bridge Creative Services Ltd
Picture Research: Hannah Taylor
and Rebecca Sodergren
Production: Duncan Gilbert

Originated by Chroma Graphics Pte. Ltd
Printed and bound in China by
South China Printing Company

13 digit ISBN 978 1 406 20332 5 (hardback)
10 09 08 07 06
10 9 8 7 6 5 4 3 2 1

13 digit ISBN 978 1 406 20339 4 (paperback)
11 10 09 08 07
10 9 8 7 6 5 4 3 2 1

**British Library Cataloguing in
Publication Data**
Thomas, Isabel, 1980–
Scorpion vs. tarantula. – (Animals head to head)
1. Tarantulas – Juvenile literature
2. Scorpions – Juvenile literature
3. Animal fighting – Juvenile literature
4. Predation (Biology) – Juvenile literature
I. Title
595.4'41566
A full catalogue record for this book is available
from the British Library.

Acknowledgements
The publishers would like to thank the following for
permission to reproduce photographs:

Alamy Images pp. **6** (Maximilian Weinzierl), **11**,
23 top (Juniors Bildarchiv), **23 bottom** (Bruce
Coleman INC), **28** (Ron Yue); Corbis pp. **15** (William
Dow), **26 left** (Tom Brakefield); DK Images p. **16**;
FLPA pp. **13** (Minden Pictures/Mark Moffett), **21**
(Minden Pictures/Mark Moffett); Getty Images
p. **12** (Photographer's Choice); Naturepl.com pp. **10**
(Richard Du Toit), **14** (Doug Wechsler), **19** (Jose B.
Ruiz); NHPA pp. **4 right** (Daniel Heuclin), **7** (Daniel
Heuclin), **8** (Anthony Bannister), **9** (Daniel Heuclin),
17 (Stephen Dalton), **24** (Daniel Heuclin), **25** (Daniel
Heuclin); Photolibrary.com p. **20**; Science Photo
Library pp. **4 left** (Pascal Goetgheluck), **18** (Tom
McHugh), **26 right** (Peter Chadwick), **29** (David
M. Schleser).

Cover photograph of scorpion reproduced
with permission of Ardea/Andy Teare. Cover
photograph of tarantula reproduced with
permission of FLPA/Minden Pictures/Gerry Ellis.

Every effort has been made to contact copyright
holders of any material reproduced in this book.
Any omissions will be rectified in subsequent
printings if notice is given to the publishers.

The paper used to print this book comes from
sustainable resources.

Disclaimer

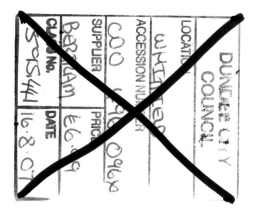

Eight-legged hunters

Scorpions and tarantulas are **arachnids**. All arachnids have eight legs and a body with two sections. Scorpions and tarantulas live in hundreds of different **habitats** around the world, from deserts to tropical rainforests. Most survive by eating insects.

Tarantulas and scorpions are known and feared as deadly hunters. But which arachnid is the champion predator? To find out, let's compare their hunting and fighting skills.

Tarantulas and scorpions live all over the world.

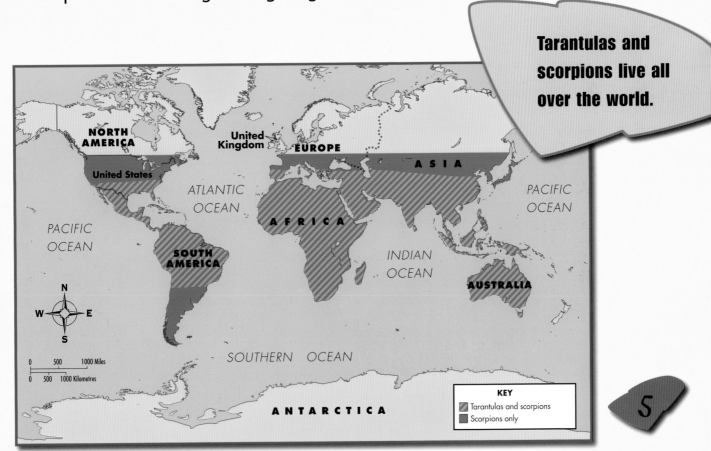

KEY
Tarantulas and scorpions
Scorpions only

Size and strength

There are at least 800 types of tarantula and 1,500 types of scorpion. Most can only catch insects, but a few are large enough to tackle snakes, birds, and even small **mammals**! The biggest **predators** have the best choice of **prey**.

Small but lethal

The smallest scorpions are just 12 millimetres (under half an inch) long. But South African and Emperor scorpions measure more than 20 centimetres (8 inches) from head to tail.

Large Emperor scorpions are popular pets!

Body: 20 cm (7.9 in)
Weight: 30-50 grams (1.0-1.8 oz)

Giant spiders

Even Emperor scorpions are small compared to the biggest tarantulas! The legs of a gigantic Goliath tarantula would reach from the top to the bottom of this page.

Goliaths live in jungles in South America. They feed on small snakes, lizards, birds, and frogs.

Tarantulas are the strongest spiders in the world. They do not need to build webs to catch prey. They just pounce on victims. Then they mash them up with powerful **mouthparts** called **chelicerae**.

Leg span: 29 cm (11 in)
Weight: 150 grams (5.3 oz)

Some tarantulas are big enough to drag baby birds out of nests.

Strength matters

A strong body helps an animal to overpower **prey** and scare enemies away.

Feeding tools

Scorpions and tarantulas both have strong **pedipalps**, which are like a pair of short legs. Tarantulas use their pedipalps to grab prey and tear it into smaller pieces.

Scorpions have longer and stronger pedipalps, with terrifying pincers on the ends. They can crush insects in seconds and give large animals a very nasty nip.

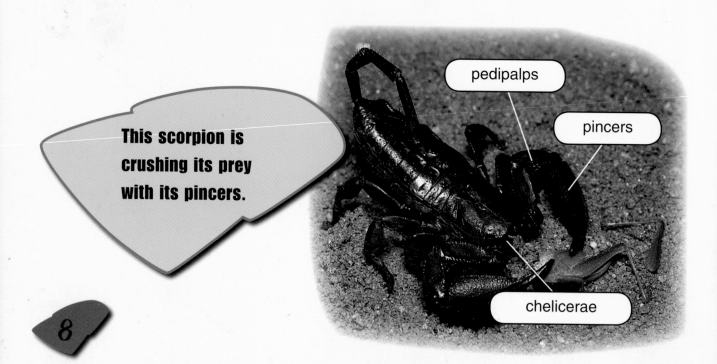

This scorpion is crushing its prey with its pincers.

pedipalps

pincers

chelicerae

Body armour

Arachnids have a hard body covering called an **exoskeleton**. It protects their bodies and stops them drying out. Every so often, tarantulas and scorpions have to wriggle out of their old exoskeleton to let their bodies grow. This is called **moulting**.

An arachnid is soft and weak after moulting. It cannot hunt or defend itself from enemies until its new exoskeleton hardens.

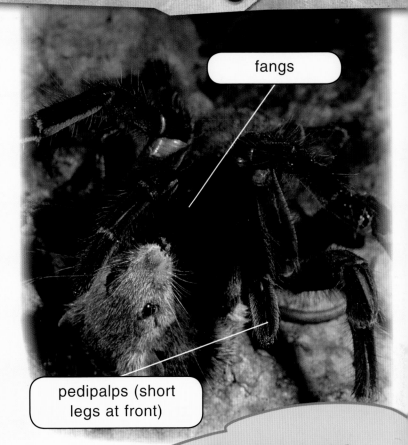

fangs

pedipalps (short legs at front)

This giant tarantula is about to sink its fangs into a mouse.

WINNER

HEAD TO HEAD

	Tarantula	Scorpion	
Size	10	7	Tarantula leaves scorpion standing in its shadow!
Strength	6	8	Scorpion uses pincers to nip ahead!

Speed and endurance

A **predator's** body is designed to catch the **prey** in its **habitat**. Tarantulas and scorpions need to move quickly to catch speedy insects.

Tarantulas usually move very slowly. But they burst into a high-speed run when chasing prey.

Scorpions also scuttle quickly when they are striking at prey or trying to escape danger. In attack, a scorpion's tail can dart forwards, sideways, or backwards extremely quickly.

Scorpions are able to run quickly to catch their prey.

10

Climbing

Some tarantulas live in trees and are excellent climbers. The ends of their legs are covered in hundreds of tiny hairs that cling to any surface. Tarantulas do not spin webs, but they use their sticky silk to hold on to **vertical** surfaces.

Small scorpions can climb walls and even walk across ceilings. But only tarantulas can climb a surface as smooth as glass.

Tarantulas can cling to smooth, shiny leaves without slipping.

Endurance

Scorpions are incredible survivors. They live everywhere from hot beaches to freezing mountains. Some can live underwater for up to two days. This means they can live in **habitats** that flood.

Scientists are amazed at scorpion survival skills. Even if a scorpion is frozen in a block of ice, it will walk away unhurt when the ice has melted!

Scorpions can live without eating for over a year if food is hard to find.

12

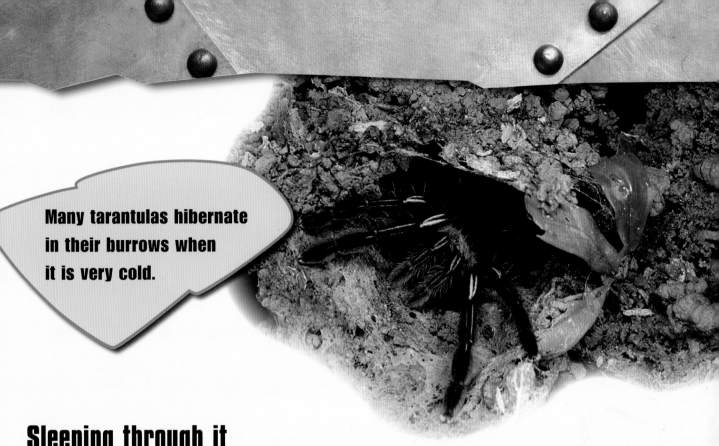

Many tarantulas hibernate in their burrows when it is very cold.

Sleeping through it

Tarantulas like to catch one meal every week in summer.
Food is harder to catch in winter, so many tarantulas **hibernate**
in their burrows. A large female can live for up to two years
without food if she doesn't use up energy by moving.

HEAD TO HEAD

WINNER

	Tarantula	Scorpion	
Speed	7	7	Tarantula sprints off but scorpion doesn't tail behind.
Endurance	9	10	Scorpion is tough enough for any conditions.

Super senses

Tarantulas and scorpions are **ambush predators**. This means they sit and wait for **prey** to come close before striking.

Many scorpions and tarantulas have colours and patterns that blend in with their **habitat**. Their prey does not notice them until it is too late!

Cunning **camouflage** helps **arachnids** to hide from their own predators too. A tarantula the colour of tree bark can sit on a tree without being spotted by hungry birds and monkeys. Many tarantulas also camouflage the entrance to their burrows.

Good camouflage helps keep tarantulas hidden.

Night hunters

Darkness is the best camouflage. Most scorpions and tarantulas are **nocturnal**. They rest in the day and come out at night to hunt.

Most scorpions are very hard to see in daylight. They blend in with their backgrounds or flatten their bodies and squeeze into tiny cracks and burrows.

At night, scorpions stay totally still so they are invisible to their prey. But scientists can spot them! **UV light** makes a scorpion's body glow in the dark.

Scorpions can't hide from scientists with a UV light!

A surprise attack!

Sharp **senses** help **arachnids** to strike at exactly the right moment.

Tarantulas and scorpions have up to eight eyes, but they cannot see shapes. Their eyes only see light and dark. This tells them when to hunt and when to hide.

Feeling hairy

Tarantulas use their amazing sense of touch to find out what is around them. They are covered in thousands of hairs that detect **vibrations**.

When **prey** moves nearby, the vibrations tell the tarantula where the victim is and how big it is. The tarantula can respond to the tiniest movement in the air.

Thousands of hairs help tarantulas to feel, smell, and taste.

Tarantulas use different types of hair to smell and taste. A male tarantula can smell a female from over a kilometre away!

Scorpion senses

A scorpion's legs and pincers are also covered with sensitive hairs. Vibrations from prey ripple through the ground and reach each of the scorpion's legs at slightly different times. This tells the scorpion where to strike.

A scorpion has sensors called pectines on its belly. No other animal has pectines. They tell the scorpion if another scorpion has walked nearby.

Using its hairs, a scorpion can feel a grain of sand that is dropped 30 cm (12 in) away.

HEAD TO HEAD

	Tarantula	Scorpion	
Camouflage	9	9	Both are masters of disguise!
Senses	8	8	Equally hard to sneak up on...

17

Deadly weapons

All **predators** have special weapons to catch and kill their **prey**. **Arachnids** use a deadly poison called **venom**. They use sharp fangs or stings to put venom into their prey.

Fang-tastic

Tarantulas have two huge fangs that are up to a centimetre long. These are strong enough to bite through human skin, and can sink easily into an insect's body. A tarantula always tries to **paralyse** an insect by biting its neck first. The tarantula does not want to be attacked by the victim's stings or pincers.

Tarantulas look menacing, but their venom is too weak to kill humans.

If an arachnid can paralyse or kill prey with a single bite or sting, it will not use up too much energy. It also avoids a noisy struggle that might attract larger predators!

Sting in the tail

A scorpion's sting contains some of the most **toxic** poisons in the world. Some of these chemicals are 100,000 times more deadly than **cyanide**.

Scorpions grip prey in their large pincers while they jab the sting into the victim's flesh. Some scorpions have such strong pincers they can crush small insects to death without having to sting them.

All scorpions can use their sting to kill prey, but only some can harm humans.

19

Death stalkers

The world's most dangerous scorpions live in Africa, the Middle East, South America, India, and Mexico.

Palestine yellow scorpions have the most poisonous **venom**. They are known as "death stalkers" because they come into houses to keep warm and dry. One sting can **paralyse** a human's heart and lungs.

Ouch!
The biggest scorpions look terrifying, but the smallest scorpions actually have more poisonous stings.

Scorpions fight and eat their own brothers and sisters if they are hungry!

It can take a tarantula days to eat one meal.

Insect soup

Arachnids digest food outside their body. Once **prey** has been killed, it is **liquefied**! Scorpions use their pincers to tear off a piece of the victim. Then they spit **digestive juices** on it and suck up the liquid mixture.

A tarantula's fangs inject digestive juices at the same time as their venom. These juices dissolve the victim's insides. They also break the venom down, so it doesn't poison the tarantula when it eats. The tarantula sucks out the insect soup, leaving a hollow shell.

HEAD TO HEAD

WINNER

	Tarantula	Scorpion	
Venom	7	10	Sting in scorpion's tail is deadly to prey and predators.
Weapons	6	10	Scorpion has a choice of weapons – sting and pincers.

21

Defence

Arachnids may be deadly to **prey**, but they are bite-sized snacks for many animals. Scorpions and tarantulas use cunning tactics to avoid being eaten.

Tactic 1: Keep still or stay hidden

Scorpions and tarantulas spend most of the day hiding in burrows or under rocks. When they leave their burrows to hunt at night, sharp **senses** tell them when a **predator** is nearby. Then they can scuttle to safety.

Playing dead

If there is nowhere to hide, scorpions stay as still as possible. Some fall into a deep sleep, as if they have been frightened to death. They come back to life after the danger has gone.

Wrestling match

When tarantulas meet in the wild they wrestle to test each other's strength. The weaker tarantula runs away.

22

Tactic 2: Scare enemies away

Some predators find tarantula burrows and dig their way in. A frightened tarantula lifts its front legs and head into the air, and shows its fangs. This warns the enemy that it is about to attack.

Goliath tarantulas scare predators by rubbing their hairy legs together. This makes a loud hissing noise that sounds like Velcro being pulled apart. It can be heard 5 metres away.

A scorpion looks threatening by holding its pincers up and arching its tail so the sting points at the enemy.

This tarantula has raised its front legs ready to defend itself.

A scorpion defends itself with its sting and its pincers.

Tarantulas flick their hairs by rubbing their legs and abdomen together.

Tactic 3: Hurt the enemy

Some brightly-coloured tarantulas from North and South America have special hairs that can be used as weapons.

Each stiff hair is coated with **venom** and has tiny hooks at the ends. The tarantula can flick thousands of these hairs into a **predator's** face.

The hairs dig into the attacker's skin, causing painful stinging. An animal might even go blind if the hairs get into its eyes.

The attacker soon learns that a brightly-coloured tarantula should not be eaten!

Some South American tarantulas have a different trick. When they are disturbed they turn away and squirt a clear liquid from behind! It smells horrible and stings the attacker's skin and eyes.

Tactic 4: Attack the enemy

The biggest tarantulas use their powerful jaws for defence. A scorpion's sting and pincers are even better weapons.

Some scorpions' normal venom is strong enough to kill or **paralyse** predators. Others make venom that causes extreme pain. This is ideal for scaring enemies away.

A scorpion can use its sting to attack animals bigger than itself.

HEAD TO HEAD

	Tarantula	Scorpion	
Scaring enemies	10	8	Tarantula gets points for trying.
Hurting enemies	8	10	Scorpion is a mean machine!

Who wins?

Sharp **senses**, armoured bodies, and deadly **venom** make tarantulas and scorpions fearsome hunters.

You've seen the evidence, but which **predator** is best? Let's imagine what might happen if they met in the wild.

Angry arachnids

The rivals would be well matched. Tarantulas are bigger and can overcome **prey** with brute force. But scorpions have deadlier venom. They could also sting without getting too close to the tarantula's dagger-like fangs.

No tarantula or scorpion likes to share its **territory** with a rival. The tarantula would raise its front legs, hiss, and spread its fangs to warn the scorpion off. The scorpion would flash its giant pincers and arch its tail forward. Then the angry **arachnids** would launch themselves at each other, struggling to bite or sting.

Hungry scorpions will fight to the death. When the tarantula realizes it could be the scorpion's next meal, it would probably sprint away and hide!

HEAD TO HEAD

	Tarantula	Scorpion
Size	10	7
Strength	6	8
Speed	7	7
Endurance	9	10
Camouflage	9	9
Senses	8	8
Venom	7	10
Weapons	6	10
Scaring enemies	10	8
Hurting enemies	8	10
Total	80/100	87/100

Scorpion is crowned the winner!

27

The real fight

Tarantulas and scorpions are good at avoiding each other in the wild. But they are at risk from a much worse enemy: humans.

Humans take tarantulas and scorpions from the wild to sell as pets or souvenirs. They destroy **arachnid habitats** by building roads and houses, and cutting down forests to grow crops. Every year thousands of tarantulas are killed as they cross roads.

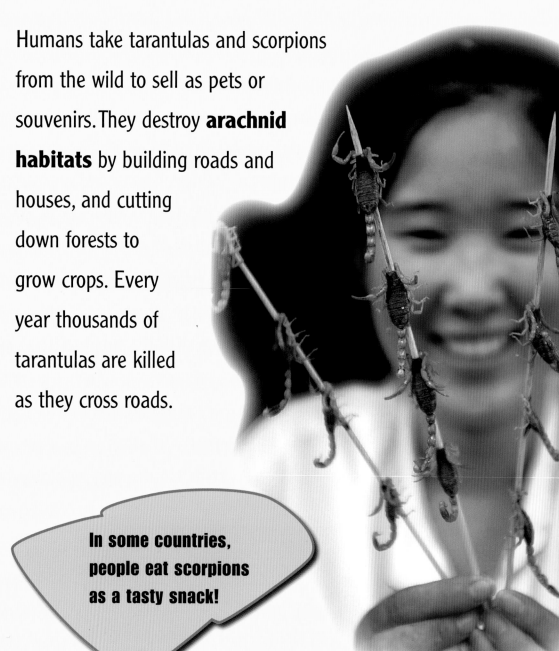

In some countries, people eat scorpions as a tasty snack!

Popular pets

Mexican red-knee tarantulas are the most popular pet spiders in the United States. So many have been collected that these tarantulas are becoming **endangered**.

Lifesavers?

Most people think of arachnids as killers, but they could also save lives. A chemical in scorpion stings can treat one type of cancer. Doctors have also discovered that a chemical in tarantula **venom** helps patients to recover from heart attacks.

It is now illegal to sell wild tarantulas.

Three types of tarantula and three types of scorpion are already endangered. If these arachnids are not protected, we may never find out what other amazing things they can do.

Glossary

abdomen back part of an arachnid's body

ambush to attack prey suddenly, from a hiding place

arachnid family of eight-legged animals, which includes tarantulas and scorpions

camouflage body features that allow animals to blend into their habitat, to avoid being seen by predators or prey

chelicerae mouthparts of an arachnid; a tarantula's chelicerae are its fangs

cyanide type of poison

digest break up food so the body can use it for energy

digestive juices liquid produced in an animal's stomach or spit to help digest food

endangered in danger of dying out altogether

exoskeleton hard body covering that supports and protects an animal's body

habitat place where an animal lives

hibernate to become less active over the winter, living off only body fat

liquefied make something become liquid

mammal animals that can make their own body heat and produce milk for their babies

moulting when an animal gets rid of its old skin and grows a new one

mouthpart body part near an insect or arachnid's mouth that is used to pick up and mash food

nocturnal active at night

paralyse stop something from moving

pedipalps leg-like mouthparts of arachnids, used for grabbing and holding prey while it is liquefied

predator animal that hunts, kills, and eats other animals

prey animal that is caught, killed, and eaten by another animal as food

senses ways in which an animal gets information about its surroundings

territory area that an animal lives in and defends against rivals

toxic can harm or kill an animal

UV light type of light

venom poisonous liquid produced by some animals to paralyse prey or defend themselves

vertical goes straight up

vibration a quick back and forth movement or shaking

More information

Books

Incredible Arachnids, John Townsend (Raintree, 2004) has amazing facts and figures about tarantulas and scorpions of all kinds.

Wild Predators: Deadly Spiders and Scorpions, Andrew Solway (Heinemann Library, 2004) explores the lives of the most dangerous arachnids.

Websites

www.thebts.co.uk – this is the home of the British Tarantula Society. Click on "galleries" and then any of the words that are highlighted in blue, to find some larger-than-life photos of multi-coloured tarantulas.

www.bbc.co.uk/reallywild – this site is packed with facts, features, and games to help you find out all about the world's amazing creatures. Follow the "amazing animals" link for more information about tarantulas.

Sizing up the scorpion and tarantula

This picture shows how big an Emperor scorpion and Mexican red-knee tarantula are, compared to a human hand.

Index